oh my soul

companion journal

ENCOUNTERING GOD

IN HONEST PRAYER

shannon guerra

Copyright © 2018 Shannon Guerra

All rights reserved. No part of this book may be reproduced in any form or by any electronic or mechanical means, including information storage and retrieval systems, without permission in writing from the publisher, except by reviewers, who may quote brief passages in a review.

ISBN 13-978-1-7325719-6-9

Scripture quotations are from the ESV® Bible (The Holy Bible, English Standard Version®), copyright © 2001 by Crossway, a publishing ministry of Good News Publishers. Used by permission. All rights reserved.

Portions of scripture in **bold** are the author's emphasis.

Cover art by Kelly Bermudez, Willow Lief Design Co.
Cover design by Copperlight Wood

This title may be purchased in bulk for educational or group study use. For more information, please email shop@copperlightwood.com.

Printed and bound in the United States of America

Published by Copperlight Wood
P.O. Box 870697
Wasilla, AK 99687

www.copperlightwood.com

contents

Introduction / 5

1   Abiding / 7

2   Identity / 17

3   Threshold / 33

4   Forward / 49

5   Friendship / 63

6   Fire / 79

7   Light / 101

Notes / 131

introduction

Confession: I am the last person in the world who should design anything involving fill-in-the-blanks, busywork, redundant questions, and time-wasting worksheets. As a homeschool mom, I'm a total failure when it comes to utilizing study guides and instruction manuals, and the last thing I need – or intend to give to anyone else – is homework.

So this is none of those.

This is your own book to write. It's for you to soak in and document your own pursuit of hearing God and talking to Him. Feel free to bend the corners, doodle in the edges, and write your own confessions, questions, requests, and intercessions, aware that He is with you and listening the whole time. Hash out the situations you're dealing with. Copy down the scripture that's speaking to you, and the answers He's giving you.

It's a journal for you to process and grow with, using only the questions and promptings that are relevant to you in this season – the ones that lead you closer to Jesus and what He's calling you to in this season. Mark the ones you use however works best for you in the circle provided next to them.

Take your time. There's no test at the end. Just more victory.

This peace is for you,

Shannon

> *The Rat pushed the paper away from him wearily, but the discreet Mole took the occasion to leave the room, and when he peeped in again sometime later, the Rat was absorbed and deaf to the world; alternately scribbling and sucking the top of his pencil. It is true that he sucked a good deal more than he scribbled; but it was joy to the Mole to know that the cure had at least begun.*
>
> - Kenneth Grahame [1]

For God alone, O my soul, wait in silence, for my hope is in Him.

- Psalm 62:5

GROWTH I'M PURSUING IN THIS SEASON:

1: abiding

The time of business does not with me differ from the time of prayer; and in the noise and clutter of my kitchen, while several persons are at the same time calling for different things, I possess God in as great tranquility as if I were upon my knees at the Blessed Sacrament.

- Brother Lawrence [1]

QUESTIONS TO CONSIDER:
○ WHAT AM I DISTRACTED BY?
○ IS THERE ANYTHING IN PARTICULAR I'M AVOIDING OR STALLING ABOUT?

It's not just our distractible nature that is roving. He is moving among us as we go about the hours of our day.

Hey, Love, He said, *when you're bored and scrolling without purpose, looking for inspiration and not finding it, it's time to look in different direction. When you're overwhelmed and looking for distraction and escape, look for Me instead. I have wonderful things to distract you with, and I will help you find your focus again.*

Your time with Me will never disappoint you. I will always leave you wiser, or rested, or both.

You don't want to miss this.

This time with Me is bountiful, potent, and effective to change and restore anything you are avoiding. This time is fertile to bring forth what you are awaiting. This time creates prolific momentum toward everything you are working for.

This time with Me is never a gamble.

You will always gain. You will always bear fruit. You will always find peace when you find Me. You will always win when you spend time with Me.

Our awareness of His presence allows Him to come between us and our agendas, and He is with us at the desk with our computers, at the table with our kids, and with us when we sleep. His peace is for you, for me, every second. [2]

QUESTIONS TO CONSIDER:

○ Is there a certain time of day when I most need to remember that God is with me?

○ What do I need to see change and restoration in?

○ What have I been praying toward that I want to see momentum in?

○ Is there any place where I haven't wanted to allow His presence to come between me and my own agenda?

_____
_____
_____
_____
_____
_____
_____
_____
_____
_____
_____
_____
_____
_____
_____
_____
_____
_____
_____
_____
_____
_____
_____
_____

I pray randomly at first, just general things: our country, our government, our kids, our town. It's not long before He brings something specific to mind.

But then I stall, hesitating – and because I am selfless and sacrificial, I tell Him, "God, I don't want to pray for that. It will just frustrate me, and I'm trying to get back to sleep."

And lightning doesn't strike me.

Instead, He says, *That's because you're doing it wrong, Love.*

Oh.

And because He is (really) selfless and sacrificial (and also, not tired) He explains it to me.

You've forgotten to pray from victory to victory, He says.

You go from glory to glory, even if the middle place is frustrating, because then you can pray from joy.

You can pray from a place of victory to a new place of even greater victory because I've already won.

And then we pray, from joy. Hope comes. [3]

QUESTIONS TO CONSIDER:

○ WHAT DO I AVOID PRAYING FOR BECAUSE IT FRUSTRATES ME OR STRESSES ME OUT?

○ WHAT WOULD THAT SITUATION LOOK LIKE IF IT WERE RESOLVED?

_____
_____
_____
_____
_____
_____
_____
_____
_____
_____
_____
_____
_____
_____

For in this hope we were saved. Now hope that is seen is not hope. For who hopes for what he sees? But if we hope for what we do not see, we wait for it with patience.

– Romans 8:24-25

When reading the Bible...

I consider reading faster. Skimming. Skipping. Trying a different chapter.
Come in anticipation, He says, *not compulsion or religious duty. Expect something. You don't need to do anything faster.*
I protest. This chapter doesn't apply to anything I'm dealing with right now.
Read anyway, He says. *Don't miss this.* 4

Questions to Consider:

○ How can I foster anticipation in my Bible reading time?

○ Am I happy with my reading routine, or do I need to make some changes? What can I do to understand the Bible better?

_____
_____
_____
_____
_____
_____

You're not distracted, He says. *You are yielded. This is a powerfully effective position to hear from Me, and I have all the answers you need.*
Your obedience to read My word steadfastly, not wavering or in fickle randomness, puts you in a posture to listen. 4

_____
_____
_____
_____
_____
_____

It's not about speed, He says. *You can't follow Me faster. It's about devotion, which cultivates abundance.*

When you are devotedly pursuing Me, your capacity turns exponential. Grace never adds up correctly. Grace multiplies. [5]

But seek first the kingdom of God and his righteousness, and all these things will be added to you.

- Matthew 6:33

QUESTIONS TO CONSIDER:
- What does God say when I pray through scripture?
- How does [choose any Psalm] change when I pray through it?

2: identity

It's a stage we all go through; it takes a certain amount of living to strike the strange balance between the two errors either of regarding ourselves as unforgivable or as not needing forgiveness.

- Madeleine L'Engle [1]

Why is simple obedience so hard?
Shame, fear, and control are merciless taskmasters. Remember?
Oh, yes. I remember. A friend and I talked about it in depth a few months ago. I sat in the passenger seat of her car while it idled in the driveway and hastily scribbled what He was telling me:
People are afraid of changing because they fear future shame, not understanding there is no shame in repentance. It's the enemy's ruse to keep them from growing closer to Me.
They only need to ask to be excused, and My grace covers them. [2]

QUESTIONS TO CONSIDER:

○ WHERE DO I TEND TO REGARD MYSELF AS UNFORGIVABLE, OR AS NOT NEEDING FORGIVENESS?

○ WHERE AM I STRUGGLING WITH OBEDIENCE?

○ AM I AFRAID OF CHANGING BECAUSE I DON'T WANT TO ADMIT I'VE BEEN WRONG?

○ WHAT WOULD FREEDOM LOOK LIKE IN THIS AREA?

_____
_____
_____
_____
_____
_____

There is no shame in repentance, only wisdom...which only fools will shun.

Oh, friends...do you need to be excused? What should you do? *Do not be ashamed of the returning...*

Pardon, release, forgiveness, and freedom come in the asking. Healing comes in the closeness. And then we can play, and rest.[3]

QUESTIONS TO CONSIDER:

◯ HAVE I BEEN ASHAMED OF RETURNING TO GOD, OR BEING CLOSE TO HIM? WHAT DOES HE SAY ABOUT THAT?

◯ WHAT WOULD HEALING LOOK LIKE IN THIS SEASON?

You were running well. Who hindered you from obeying the truth?

– Galatians 5:7

Resentment, bitterness, unforgiveness, and refusal to accept responsibility are grave hindrances to our effectiveness in prayer. They are rocks we trip over, boulders we butt up against, and we wonder why our prayers seem to go nowhere. Sometimes it's because we've let things pile up, and they've cemented right in the middle of the path we're walking.

But they don't have to stay there.

Therefore, confess your sins to one another and pray for one another, that you may be healed. The prayer of a righteous person has great power as it is working.

– James 5:16

Humility and repentance are the gentle dynamite that clear our path. It's not that He doesn't hear us, or doesn't want *xyz* and the rest of the whole crazy alphabet for us. Sometimes, we've got some unfinished business to attend to first.[4]

QUESTIONS TO CONSIDER:

○ HAVE I BEEN TRIPPING OVER ANY RESENTMENT, BITTERNESS, UNFORGIVENESS, OR REFUSAL TO ACCEPT RESPONSIBILITY?

○ WHAT DOES GOD WANT FOR ME IN THIS STAGE OF LIFE?

_____
_____
_____
_____
_____
_____
_____
_____
_____

There have been prayers I've avoided because they were about issues I didn't want to deal with. I thought that once I mentioned it to God, it would be this giant can of worms and I'd be up all night hashing things out and crying ugly tears and going to therapy for the next six months.

But no. Oh, no. I mean, sometimes those things are necessary, but not usually. He's much more efficient than that.

Once I gave in, at the speed of thought He was right there to bring truth, wisdom, conviction, healing. In a flash, a transaction of forgiveness occurred – from Him to me, from me to others. It happens swiftly when we let Him. Posthaste. Immediately.

We've been trying to teach our kids this as we learn it ourselves: He speaks in the surrender.

He is gentle and forgiving where we are stubborn and hard, and He helps us to be brave, transparent, unafraid to face responsibility, and move on.[5]

QUESTIONS TO CONSIDER:

◯ WHAT HAVE I AVOIDED PRAYING ABOUT BECAUSE I DIDN'T WANT TO ADDRESS IT?

◯ WHAT DOES GOD REALLY SAY ABOUT THAT SITUATION?

> **But God,** *being rich in mercy, because of the great love with which he loved us, even when we were dead in our trespasses,* **made us alive** *together with Christ—by grace* **you have been saved—** *and* **raised us up with him** *and* **seated us with him in the heavenly places** *in Christ Jesus.*
>
> - Ephesians 2:4-6

I'm still a work in progress. Metamorphosis is painful, and probably the most significant way I can tell He's maturing me is that now I let Him work in spite of the pain.[6]

QUESTIONS TO CONSIDER:

○ HOW HAVE I BEEN MADE ALIVE? WHERE HAS GOD BROUGHT RESURRECTION TO OLD PLACES IN MY LIFE THAT WERE DEAD?

○ HOW IS HE STILL MATURING ME IN THIS SEASON?

It might be good if we stopped using the terms "victory" and "defeat" to describe our progress of holiness. Rather we should use the terms "obedience" and "disobedience."

- Jerry Bridges [7]

    We feel the struggle, strain, and pain on the upward climb, not the downhill slope. We are breathless from the effort that achieves progress, not the easy plateau. [8]

QUESTIONS TO CONSIDER:

- HOW DOES THIS CHANGE HOW I VIEW MY PROGRESS?
- HOW DOES CORRECTING MY VIEW OF PROGRESS IMPACT MY INTIMACY WITH GOD? HOW DOES IT AFFECT MY CONTINUED PROGRESS?

Regarding Shame:

One of the enemy's tactics is to take something that just needs a small correction and blow it out of proportion in our hearts – to convince us that *we* are bad, instead of the sin or the mistake. He paints with a broad brush, trying to tell us the entire thing and everything associated with the situation or event was wrong and humiliating.

> *The thief comes only to steal and kill and destroy. I came that they may have life and have it abundantly.*
>
> *- John 10:10*

Questions to Consider:

○ Is there any area of my life that has been restricted by shame?

○ What would it look like to have God replace shame with His truth and life?

_____
_____
_____
_____
_____
_____
_____
_____
_____
_____
_____
_____
_____
_____
_____

Every year, we're not who we used to be. By His grace we're more like who we're meant to be.

God cares about you and your situation – your past, and your future. And any mess that you are in right now? He has good plans for it. Not a thing is wasted.

You are the best, you-est you as you move further into the future He has for you. Still you, but refined. Golden. Blooming, with new wings. 9

From now on, therefore, we regard no one according to the flesh. Even though we once regarded Christ according to the flesh, we regard him thus no longer. Therefore, if anyone is in Christ, he is a new creation. The old has passed away; behold, the new has come. All this is from God, who through Christ reconciled us to himself and gave us the ministry of reconciliation.

– 2 Corinthians 5:16-18

Most of us can run from our past, but it takes strength to face it, sift through the rubble, and let God wash through it.

The enemy wants us to be cowards: weak, and easily manipulated. Any wretch can deny, lie, or persist in wrong thinking or wrong behavior. It takes guts to turn your face toward light when you've been hiding in shadows.

It takes a special kind of bravery to admit fault, be teachable, and turn. It takes grit and valor to start over.

I thank him who has given me strength, Christ Jesus our Lord, because he judged me faithful, appointing me to his service, though formerly I was a blasphemer, persecutor, and insolent opponent. But I received mercy because I had acted ignorantly in unbelief, and the grace of our Lord overflowed for me with the faith and love that are in Christ Jesus.

- 1 Timothy 1:12-14

Tabula rasa. It's okay – sometimes it's even best – to start over. He won't waste a thing. [10]

Rudeness only looks like dislike of others, He told me, *though it usually has nothing to do with their feelings about someone else. It has to do with their vision of themselves. And manners, too…but mostly it's how they see themselves, and how they see Me.*

He tells us, *You have more than you can imagine. When you look in the mirror, sometimes you hardly know that person. You have no idea who you're dealing with.* [11]

QUESTIONS TO CONSIDER:

○ WHAT DISTORTED IMAGES/REFLECTIONS HAVE I ACCEPTED AS TRUTH ABOUT MYSELF? ABOUT GOD?

○ HOW MIGHT A CORRECT VIEW OF MYSELF AND GOD IMPACT THE WAY I RELATE TO OTHERS?

You have no idea who you're dealing with, He told me. Not threatening, but gently patient. *Who you're dealing with is Myself, and yourself, in ways you've never known or seen before.*

About Himself, He said, *I love you more than you can imagine. I am bigger than you can imagine. You have no idea Who you're dealing with. I want to show you, so you can show others.*

It's the time of fruition, of fullness, He said. *This is the time for reaching upwards and outwards, boldly expressing My truth and love in a way that is wilder than you have ever done before. It is the right time now. It may be untamed, but I want to be set loose in your life without encumbrance or inhibition.*

He's given you a way to express His love and truth in a way that might surprise you.

It has...everything to do with getting rid of the weight of our past and reminding us of desires and dreams we have for the future.

We thought they were just passing fancies or crazy daydreams.

But He's saying, *No. I'm serious.* [12]

QUESTIONS TO CONSIDER:

◯ HOW IS GOD CALLING ME TO EXPRESS HIS TRUTH AND LOVE IN WAYS THAT ARE WILDER THAN I'VE EVER DONE BEFORE?

◯ WHAT MIGHT IT LOOK LIKE FOR GOD TO BE SET LOOSE IN MY LIFE IN THESE WAYS? WHAT WOULD FRUITION AND FULLNESS LOOK LIKE?

◯ WHAT DAYDREAMS HAVE I HAD THAT GOD MIGHT BE SERIOUS ABOUT?

_____
_____
_____
_____
_____
_____
_____

3: threshold

I'm tired, and in the middle of the night my to-do list looks so magnified that I feel done in before the day has even had a chance to start.

Hey, Love, He says. *Your night vision is inflating your problems. Try a different point of view: Magnify Me instead. Picture the victory.* [1]

...in the presence of the God in whom he believed, who gives life to the dead and calls into existence the things that do not exist.

- Romans 4:17b

Therefore I tell you, whatever you ask in prayer, believe that you have received it, and it will be yours.

- Mark 11:24

And Jesus answered them, "Truly, I say to you, if you have faith and do not doubt, you will not only do what has been done to the fig tree, but even if you say to this mountain, 'Be taken up and thrown into the sea,' it will happen. And whatever you ask in prayer, you will receive, if you have faith."

- Matthew 21:21-22

QUESTIONS TO CONSIDER:

○ WHAT ARE THE BREAKTHROUGHS I'M PRAYING TOWARD?

○ WHAT DOES VICTORY LOOK LIKE FOR EACH OF THEM?

_____

_____

_____

_____

_____

_____

_____

I picture the victory of special needs healed, casting mountains to the sea, because He can. Because He wants to teach me how, and He wants me to remember to do it instead of feeding anxiety and letting it wreak havoc.

The day ahead becomes do-able. Fretting and fears diminished. Faith and hope rising.

It's more than just my feelings – the future has changed. We are the clean-up operation, working the night shift. [2]

On "decaf thoughts" (complaints and things we stress out over):

They're heavy-yoked, drowsy, and splashing all over the place. Not particularly productive, not creating momentum.

The big and little events of the day can shake us or they can stir us. We can respond with dull lethargy or be stirred to unceasing prayer that is productive, creative, and fruitful, instead of just reacting to life around us. [3]

Questions to consider:

- What do I tend to complain about and stress out over?
- How can I convert those thoughts to productive prayer?
- Is there someone I can confide in to help keep me accountable in this?

I'm still working on picturing the victory. He said, *Don't think of where it is right now – that's the floor. Think of the ceiling.*

Pray from joy, from victory to victory. From floor to ceiling, and then the next level up. There's always more.

I can do this for a million things. My efforts as a mother, a friend, a writer, a wife; healing for our kids, our hearts, our loved ones. 4

So I start telling Him all about it: Where we've come from, where we're at, where we're going, and where I want to be.

He says, *That's a great start.*

That's only My floor, though. There's so much more. 4

> *Now to him who is **able to do far more abundantly than all that we ask or think,** according to the power at work within us, to him be glory in the church and in Christ Jesus throughout all generations, forever and ever. Amen.*
>
> *- Ephesians 3:20-21*

QUESTIONS TO CONSIDER:

○ WHERE HAVE I COME FROM? WHERE AM I AT? WHERE AM I GOING, AND WHERE DO I WANT TO BE?

○ WHAT "MORE" MIGHT GOD HAVE FOR ME BEYOND THAT?

Praying does not let us off the hook in serving others, getting involved, giving extravagantly, or anything else that gets our hands dirty. Our mission is firmly outside the comfort zone.

What unceasing prayer will do is give us greater wisdom for how He wants us to accomplish those things, which eliminates much of the anxiety and discomfort that doing them might cause otherwise. And this is important, because He will ask us to do things that feel bigger than we are. [5]

Sometimes He asks us to do something that seems like it's not "you." What if His prompting feels too intimidating, too unfamiliar, too hard, too new?

It can be a big or a little thing....That thing we can't stop thinking about but feels out of reach, or that Next Big Thing that we keep pushing to the back of our minds because we have no idea how to begin it. And we're nervous about talking to someone about it or even praying about it because, well, when you do that, things might get a little more serious... and we're not so sure we want it to be serious. [6]

QUESTIONS TO CONSIDER:

○ WHAT FEELS OUT OF REACH, BUT I CAN'T STOP THINKING ABOUT IT?

○ WHAT HAVE I PUSHED TO THE BACK OF MY MIND BECAUSE I DON'T KNOW WHAT THE NEXT STEP IS?

And He tells us, *Oh, Love...who do you think you are, anyway?*
Don't you really want to know who you are? Because you're so much more than who you limit yourself to be inside the safety of your comfort zone.

This habit of relentless prayer broadens the limits that we set for ourselves. Little steps become big steps. Those big steps get easier and start to feel like little steps. And before you know it, your comfort zone has grown deep and wide and you're still pushing the edges of it outward. [6]

QUESTIONS TO CONSIDER:

◯ WHAT AM I AFRAID OF OUTSIDE THE COMFORT ZONE?

◯ WHO AM I INSIDE THE COMFORT ZONE? WHO AM I OUTSIDE OF IT?

◯ WHAT IF I TRUSTED GOD TO PROTECT ME OUTSIDE THE COMFORT ZONE AS IT EXPANDS AROUND ME?

Times are hard in some places. The enemy threatens without and within, which is all the more reason to retaliate with a bigger vision. Ignore the hiss of the snake and start writing anyway.

Ugliness is out there, work needs to be done, and healing needs to come. It's because of this that we so badly need to listen. He dreams over us. We get to partner with Him in making the days ahead better simply by believing Him and then acting like it.

We write everything down, and it goes from some airy, tenuous vision to something defined, wrapped up in words. [7]

He has questions for me, for us.
If it didn't matter what anyone else thought…
If it didn't matter who noticed…
If it didn't matter who paid attention…
What would you let Me do in your life? [8]

How would you let Me move?
Where would you let Me take you?

I can write a list and come up with all kinds of crazy ideas, but for them to become more than just words on paper I have to give Him permission to move in me, through me, around me. And when I think of what that means, it's a little Be Careful What You Ask For-ish.

He asks us, *Can I carry you over the threshold?* [8]

But what if we don't know which way to go? What if our threshold is more like a fork in the road?

God...just tell me. Which way? Do I focus on this thing, or that thing? We ask for doors to open, doors to shut, and when we go to check, they're swinging back and forth on their hinges. This isn't what I asked for.

He says, *What did you ask for, Love?*

And I think, oh...nothing much. Just an answer – a clear answer. A neon sign. Something really bright with flashing arrows would be just about perfect.

I don't usually use those. Especially when *I already told you what to do.* [9]

QUESTIONS TO CONSIDER:

○ WHAT HAS GOD ALREADY TOLD ME TO DO?

○ IS IT SOMETHING I NEED TO START, OR JUST CONTINUE DOING FOR NOW?

*He said, "But I will be with you, and **this shall be the sign for you**, that I have sent you: **when you have brought the people out of Egypt**, [obeyed in doing what I already told you to do] you shall serve God on this mountain."*

– Exodus 3:12

*And **when the soles of the feet** of the priests bearing the ark of the Lord, the Lord of all the earth, **shall rest in the waters of the Jordan, the waters of the Jordan shall be cut off from flowing**, and the waters coming down from above shall stand in one heap."*

– Joshua 3:13

Step in. You have to get your feet wet first. Walk where I tell you, and then watch Me hold the waters back.

Sometimes confirmation comes after obedience, not before. God is not a micromanager. If His instructions are clear but we're still asking for confirmation, our problem is probably not in knowing His will – it's in following through and doing His will. The waters won't move for us while we stall at the shoreline. [10]

_____
_____
_____
_____
_____
_____
_____
_____
_____
_____
_____
_____
_____
_____
_____

The issues are delicate and lives are at stake. We plunge in with caution – quick to obey, but careful to clean up our own hearts before all else.

I'll show you what to focus on first, He said. *It's right in front of you.*

When you realize that your own heart and obedience are the first thing to deal with, you are protected from being overwhelmed and stupefied. Surrender gives you a calm simplicity to just do the first thing, and then the next thing. Simple steps, consistent prayer, steady progress. [11]

And without faith it is impossible to please him, for whoever would draw near to God must believe that he exists and that he rewards those who seek him.

- Hebrews 11:6

By faith Abraham obeyed when he was called to go out to a place that he was to receive as an inheritance. And he went out, **not knowing where he was going.**

- Hebrews 11:8

4: forward

You have what you need to walk through safely, He says. You just have to remember how to operate it.

The crockpot does nothing when it's turned off; neither does my faith when I waver.

> *In all circumstances take up the shield of faith, with which you can extinguish all the flaming darts of the evil one.*
>
> - Ephesians 6:16

I've given you a picture of the victory, Love. Hold it high.
That faith – that vision, picturing the victory He has ahead – is our shield. It covers and protects our families and our marriages. And it is really, crucially, super important. [1]

QUESTIONS TO CONSIDER:

○ WHAT ARE SOME OF THE DARTS THAT HAVE BEEN COMING AT ME?

○ HOW CAN I BETTER OPERATE MY SHIELD OF FAITH IN THIS SEASON?

_____
_____
_____
_____
_____
_____
_____
_____
_____
_____
_____
_____
_____

_____
_____
_____
_____
_____
_____
_____
_____
_____
_____
_____
_____
_____

What terrifies others is becoming ho-hum to you because you've let Me move through you. Let Me surprise you with how much I am making you capable of.

Those who are on the front lines of a battle come under the heaviest fire, He reminds me often. *But I am your covering. I am above and below, before you and behind you, and in you to do strong, mighty things. I have your back.* [2]

QUESTIONS TO CONSIDER:

○ WHAT THINGS HAVE BECOME HO-HUM TO ME AS I'VE ALLOWED GOD TO MOVE THROUGH ME?

○ WHAT ARE THE NEXT FEW STEPS THAT ARE PUSHING ME OUT OF MY COMFORT ZONE?

_____
_____
_____
_____
_____
_____

I wonder if any of Moses' people really knew what was coming after the raging was over. I wonder when Moses finally believed it, for real.

They were going to be stronger, bigger.

They were going to be free, flourishing. Alive.

> *And Moses said to the people, "Fear not, stand firm, and see the salvation of the Lord, which He will work for you today. For the Egyptians whom you see today, you shall never see again. The Lord will fight for you, and you have only to be silent."*
>
> *The Lord said to Moses, "Why do you cry to me? Tell the people of Israel to go forward."*
>
> *- Exodus 14:13-15*

He tells us something, too. And it, too, is personal:
Tell the people to go forward.
Prepare to be delivered. [3]

QUESTIONS TO CONSIDER:

◯ WHAT MIGHT IT LOOK LIKE TO BE DELIVERED IN MY CURRENT CIRCUMSTANCES?

◯ IS THERE ANY WAY I'M RESISTING THAT DELIVERANCE?

_____
_____
_____
_____
_____
_____
_____
_____
_____
_____
_____
_____

*Now to him who is **able to do far more abundantly than all that we ask or think**, according to the power at work within us, to him be glory in the church and in Christ Jesus throughout all generations, forever and ever. Amen.*

- *Ephesians 3:20-21*

But when he saw the wind, he was afraid, and beginning to sink he cried out, "Lord, save me." Jesus immediately reached out his hand and took hold of him, saying to him, "O you of little faith, why did you doubt?"

- Matthew 14:30-31

He saw the wind, and then he was afraid. And then he started to sink.

He wasn't sinking before. His fear induced the sinking. It was, literally, that sinking, dropping feeling.

When Peter walked on water toward Me, he was afraid of the wind. It was just a bunch of hot air.

The enemy is full of it. Hot air, I mean.

We can't hold high the shield of faith while entertaining fear at the same time. It's only one or the other, and both will cause something to happen. We have to choose. [4]

QUESTIONS TO CONSIDER:

◯ WHAT SITUATIONS AM I DEALING WITH THAT MIGHT BE ONLY THE WIND?

◯ WHAT DO I STAND TO LOSE IF I CHOOSE FEAR? WHAT DO I STAND TO GAIN IF I CHOOSE FAITH?

_____
_____
_____
_____
_____
_____
_____
_____
_____
_____
_____
_____

Doubt and his ugly friends stand as shadows obscuring our vision of reality. They want us to see the job loss, but not the opportunity right around the corner. They want to show off the conflict, but not the deeper wisdom that results from it. They want to illuminate the wrinkles, but make you forget about the character and experience that came with those lines. Whatever fiction doubt tries to sell us, it's never the full story. [5]

> *Through [Jesus] we have also obtained access by faith into this grace in which we stand, and we rejoice in hope of the glory of God.*
>
> *Not only that, but we rejoice in our sufferings, knowing that suffering produces endurance, and endurance produces character, and character produces hope, and hope does not put us to shame, because God's love has been poured into our hearts through the Holy Spirit who has been given to us.*
>
> *– Romans 5:2-5*

QUESTIONS TO CONSIDER:

- WHAT OPPORTUNITY IS RIGHT AROUND THE CORNER?
- WHAT DEEPER WISDOM AM I LEARNING IN THE CHALLENGES I'M FACING? WHAT KIND OF CHARACTER AM I DEVELOPING?
- WHAT DOES IT LOOK LIKE FOR ME TO "REJOICE IN HOPE OF THE GLORY OF GOD" RIGHT NOW?

There's always more beneath the surface. He moves through our prayer more than we see or know. Sometimes we're stripped of leaves and comfort, but it's not because He's finished with us – it's because He has a whole new covering ready for us in the next season. [5]

Therefore, my beloved brothers, be steadfast, immovable, always abounding in the work of the Lord, knowing that in the Lord your labor is not in vain.

– 1 Corinthians 15:58

We need His truth in circumstances that are raw, tender, and confusing, so we can know how to pray life back into them. [6]

PRAYING LIFE BACK INTO MY CIRCUMSTANCES:

_____
_____
_____
_____
_____
_____
_____
_____
_____
_____
_____
_____
_____
_____
_____
_____
_____
_____
_____
_____
_____
_____
_____
_____
_____

The truth is, sometimes we choose to walk right into the storm because we've been called on duty for a rescue operation. Other times it's because we've made a wrong turn, or it might be that we're just under attack. In any case, we have a choice to make that will affect the level of aftermath we deal with later.

He reminds me over and over: *It's not about avoiding the storm. It's about whether or not you will trust Me so I can partner with you in it.*

We can either fear the storm and its outcome, or trust the One who tells it to be still as we move with Him in the midst of it. The end of the story will be different depending on that choice. When we entertain fear, we align with it. When we entertain faith, we align with it. It's that serious.

Fear is not a feeling; it is an attack to be fought off. It is a spirit:

> *For God gave us a spirit **not of fear** but of power and love and self-control.*
>
> *- 2 Timothy 1:7*

Fear and worry are not the same thing as wise preparation and they will never ensure safety. [6]

This is serious. *Do not fear* is a command, not a suggestion, for good reason. Fear doesn't care for permission; it just wants access. The counterfeit picture of what we're afraid of may be the key that permits that access.

But agreeing with God, picturing the victory and trusting Him for what He has promised, strips the enemy of power he will wrest from us otherwise. Trusting God is the fatal, final blow that puts fear out of our misery. [7]

QUESTIONS TO CONSIDER:

- HOW HAVE I BEEN FIGHTING FEAR LATELY?
- HOW CAN I AGREE WITH GOD IN THESE SITUATIONS?
- WHAT DOES TRUSTING HIM LOOK LIKE RIGHT NOW?

We cannot use our imagination to create a picture of all the possible evils that might occur in any given situation. It's not just worrying; it's a temptation we must resist because our very lives are at stake.

The burden we carry – the light yoke – is to refuse to carry the heavy burden fear tries to place on us. We have powerful tools not only to keep fear from trespassing, but to dispatch it entirely:

Tell fear No Soliciting. Play it cool.
Reject anything it tries to sell you.
Hold high the picture of victory that I've given you.

Hope is a powerful fuel, and when combined with truth, it turns fear, doubt, despair, and discouragement to ashes. Our prayer is a bellows, breathing oxygen everywhere the fire needs to be kindled. [8]

In current events, in the headlines, in our family, in our uncertainty – as we are pursuing Him, He is positioning us and the events around us into specific alignment and formation.

He hasn't misplaced us. He is preparing us.

Every historic notable, every Biblical figure, every literary hero had a point when it felt like things were crashing down, when things weren't working out and were going downhill fast. They felt like they'd blown it.

In literature it's called climax, but in reality it has nothing to do with a literary formula. It is that people who lead quiet, conventional, easy lives never changed history. Epics aren't written about people who lived in mediocre normalcy. [9]

Fear is replaced with a determination – grim, if necessary – that we are here, in this time, for a strategic purpose. That purpose is to be met, not run from and feared. We must recognize it, even if it's called a name that we had forgotten. Even if it takes us to a place we didn't expect. He's bringing things into focus to show us that He has been here all along.

Plow forward. Lean in, steady on.

He's putting us in our place…and it's a good one. It's a position of influence, of strategy, and of impact. We're not lost. We're not losing it.
We are leading. [10]

Questions to consider:

○ What is my purpose right now? How am I moving forward to meet it?

○ Looking back, how can I see that God has been positioning and preparing me for this?

_____
_____
_____
_____
_____
_____
_____
_____
_____
_____
_____
_____
_____
_____
_____
_____
_____

5: friendship

I was totally discouraged. Didn't want to write. Didn't want to wait or listen. Didn't want to be transparent, because what I was seeing and feeling was not flattering. Didn't want to, you can't make me, stomp and huff.

But then He sent words from friends. A gift.

You are loved, He says. *Pray without ceasing, write without quitting, and love without boundaries, because you need each other.* [1]

QUESTIONS TO CONSIDER:

○ WHO CAN I BE VULNERABLE WITH? WHO CAN PICTURE THE VICTORY FOR ME BECAUSE THEY KNOW THE THINGS I STRUGGLE WITH?

○ WHEN HAS GOD UNEXPECTEDLY USED A FRIEND TO PULL ME OUT OF DISCOURAGEMENT? HOW DID IT CHANGE MY PERSPECTIVE ON MY SITUATION?

○ HOW CAN I MAKE MYSELF MORE AVAILABLE TO BE USED IN THIS WAY FOR OTHERS?

_____
_____
_____
_____
_____
_____
_____
_____
_____
_____

Sometimes I am the friend who gets to give the gift. Around the same time, He gave me these words for someone: *Grasp the hope that is substantial, not airy. It has substance and weight to it.* But the words were for me, too.

I was fighting despair over a hard situation, and He reminded me that my thoughts are to look ahead and trust Him, knowing (because it is certain!) that He is making all things new and bringing life into dark places. When I believe otherwise, I'm allowing the enemy to trespass, to hinder me from obeying the truth and walking in joy. [1]

QUESTIONS TO CONSIDER:

○ WHAT IS THE DIFFERENCE BETWEEN "SUBSTANTIAL" AND "AIRY" HOPE?

○ HOW HAVE I SEEN GOD MAKE ALL THINGS NEW AND BRING LIFE INTO DARK PLACES?

○ HOW MIGHT TRUSTING HIM TO CONTINUE DOING THIS (EVEN WHEN I CAN'T SEE EVIDENCE OF IT), IMPACT THE CULTURE IN OUR FAMILY, CHURCH, AND COMMUNITY?

Our hope is a real thing that has thickness and heft. It has density and can be carried. It is our calling to carry it and not give the enemy power by believing the fears he tries to put in our way.

Often, we carry it for each other. We have each other's back, because the enemy plays dirty.

Friendship is a gift with a mighty purpose, He says. *Picture the victory not just for yourselves, but for each other. Expect it.* [2]

QUESTIONS TO CONSIDER:

○ HOW CAN I CARRY HOPE FOR A FRIEND RIGHT NOW?

○ HOW CAN I PICTURE THE VICTORY FOR THEM, TOO?

And let us not grow weary of doing good, for in due season we will reap, if we do not give up. So then, as we have opportunity, let us do good to everyone, and especially to those who are of the household of faith.

- Galatians 6:9-10

Hey Love, you are able to create and increase courage in each other by your words, your prayers, and your actions. Speak what is true. Pray without ceasing. Cast mountains to the sea.

So much is at stake in these small acts. They are often the aegis and covering that keeps someone from giving up before the victory comes. [2]

Then Joshua rose early in the morning and they set out from Shittim. And they came to the Jordan, he and all the people of Israel, and lodged there before they passed over. At the end of three days the officers went through the camp and commanded the people, **"As soon as you see the ark of the covenant of the Lord your God being carried by the Levitical priests, then you shall set out from your place and follow it."**

– Joshua 3:1-3

Sometimes our obedience and boldness is the sign God has placed for someone else to see. At such a time as this, our willingness may be what they are watching for. [3]

QUESTIONS TO CONSIDER:

○ WHO HAS INSPIRED ME TOWARD BOLD OBEDIENCE, AND HOW DID THEY DO IT?

○ WHO AM I DISCIPLING OR MENTORING, AND HOW AM I LEADING THEM IN OBEDIENCE AND BOLDNESS?

_____
_____
_____
_____
_____
_____
_____
_____
_____
_____
_____
_____
_____
_____

Friendship rooted in prayer, challenging us to obedience, is a powerful force to be reckoned with. The enemy takes notice and shrinks back:

> *As soon as all the kings of the Amorites who were beyond the Jordan to the west, and all the kings of the Canaanites who were by the sea, heard that the Lord had dried up the waters of the Jordan for the people of Israel until they had crossed over,* ***their hearts melted and there was no longer any spirit in them because of the people of Israel.***
>
> *– Joshua 5:1*

We need each other. A united front creates a force to be reckoned with.

You need to pray for each other, He says. *It is your greatest weapon against darkness and your greatest defense against the enemy. You need to pray with and for each other as much as possible, prayer that goes deep and wide and perhaps unnoticed by the recipient, but altogether effective nonetheless.* [4]

You need to show grace to each other and trust that I am speaking to each of you. Your effectiveness diminishes in proportion to your friendly fire.

I've called you to increase courage in each other because you will need it. If you are not speaking life and victory over each other, you are in retreat.

When you are united, your impact is exponential. This is where you find the victory. 5

QUESTIONS TO CONSIDER:

○ WHO DO I NEED TO SHOW GRACE TO? HOW CAN I SPEAK LIFE AND VICTORY OVER THEM?

○ HOW CAN I CONTRIBUTE TO A CULTURE OF A UNITED FRONT AMONG MY FRIENDSHIPS?

_____
_____
_____
_____
_____
_____
_____
_____
_____
_____
_____
_____
_____
_____
_____
_____
_____
_____

It is weeks, months since we wrote that list and agreed to walk through the threshold, and I'm still unsure about how to tackle everything in the big picture.

I'll give you everything you need, He says. *It won't always be what you expect.*

Often, I'll give it to you in the form of other people. Otherwise you would think you could do it all on your own, and eventually, you would think you could do it without Me.

I'm putting just the right people in your path to walk with you, He says. *I'm also putting you in the path of others, to walk with them. But hey, Love...do not always expect a leisurely stroll to the mailbox.* [6]

QUESTIONS TO CONSIDER:

○ WHO HAS GOD PUT IN MY PATH TO HELP ME GET THIS FAR? WHAT DO I STILL NEED IN ORDER TO WALK THROUGH MY THRESHOLD?

○ WHAT CAN I OFFER TO OTHERS TO HELP THEM WALK THROUGH THEIR THRESHOLDS?

I am the vine; you are the branches. Whoever abides in me and I in him, he it is that bears much fruit, for apart from me you can do nothing.

- John 15:5

We know this verse so well it threatens to numb us in familiarity. We know that we bear fruit when we abide in his presence. We pay so much attention to this that sometimes we overlook the other role of branches that are connected to the vine: they are a covering for those who seek refuge.

We run to him, the Vine, so we can be His hands and feet to others when they come to us. Branches are a shelter and the vulnerable run to them for protection. [7]

QUESTIONS TO CONSIDER:

- HOW HAVE I EXPERIENCED REFUGE AMONG GOD'S PEOPLE?
- HOW CAN I OFFER THIS REFUGE AND COVERING FOR OTHERS?

We are that for others, they are that for us. Friends, family, church, and home are the emotional shelters we cultivate for each other — these are the relationships where we nurse our wounds and rest after a hard day. They're the school that teaches and grows us, and sometimes, they're our emergency room.

It's not a tangible place, but a spiritual safety we create for others in our relationships. It is where love is tended and fruit is borne. It is where life is protected. [7]

Sometimes we get lost in the wilderness. And He is our refuge, of course — but in His abundant generosity, He also gives us friends to confirm His wisdom and to comfort us as we navigate the dark forest.

Oh, how abundant is your goodness, which you have stored up for those who fear you and worked for those who take refuge in you, in the sight of the children of mankind!

In the cover of your presence you hide them from the plots of men; you store them in your shelter from the strife of tongues.

- Psalm 31:19-20

For over two years I went through a dark season, plowing through expectations, obligations, the feeling of never doing enough, never being enough, and not having the time or emotional margin to do more than walk around in circles. I knew that grace was there, but I couldn't see it; I knew that I was supposed to feel free, but instead I felt fried.

But my friends could see it for me. Those closest to me spoke freedom into me when I didn't have the words for myself. [8]

QUESTIONS TO CONSIDER:

○ AM I STRUGGLING WITH EMOTIONAL MARGIN, OVERWHELM, AND FEELINGS OF NOT BEING/DOING/HAVING ENOUGH? WHEN I TALK TO GOD ABOUT IT, WHAT DOES HE SAY?

○ WHO CAN I TRUST TO SPEAK FREEDOM INTO ME WHEN I CAN'T HEAR IT FOR MYSELF? HOW CAN I TELL THEY'RE A GOOD SOURCE OF TRUTH? HAVE I GIVEN THEM PERMISSION TO SPEAK FREELY WITH ME?

○ HOW CAN I SPEAK FREEDOM INTO THOSE GOING THROUGH A DARK SEASON AROUND ME?

_____
_____
_____
_____
_____

We need each other's point of view so we can have each other's back. Through our prayers, our friendship, and our words, we shield those around us from harm. We comfort them when they're hurting and create a safe place to rest and grow as they seek Him. Our friendships are the haven, the hospice, and occasionally the theater that provides comic relief and satire after a hard day.

He made us to be a covering for each other.

We don't stay there constantly. There's a whole forest to be tended, loved, and known as we reach out to provide the comfort He gives us to the communities around us. Sometimes we're the temporary hostel for acquaintances and strangers just passing through. Other times we're the chapel.

But we do come back to our own nest in the bracken — these close relationships that nurture us — to rest, reassess, and recuperate. [9]

In the embracing light and warmth, warm and dry at last, with weary legs propped up in front of them, and a suggestive clink of plates being arranged on the table behind, it seemed to the storm-driven animals, now in safe anchorage, that the cold and trackless Wild Wood just left outside was miles and miles away, and all that they had suffered in it a half-forgotten dream.

- Kenneth Grahame [10]

6: fire

Situations intensify and loom over us, requiring more than elbow grease and a checkbook to finish off.

This kind of stuff doesn't fit neatly on a to-do list: Hard relationships. Hard decisions. Health issues, deadlines, changes, and clutter. You know the ones – those things that float around, making mental noise and disorder. They're not even all bad; mostly, they're just taking up far more space than any one situation rightfully should, like a two-year-old with a mocha. It's not that the concerns aren't real or don't need to be addressed. But stacked on top of each other, they magnify way out of proportion from stress, exhaustion, and fear. Negative words from within and without cast each issue on the wall in an intimidating shadow, a projected image that is much bigger than what reality actually deals us. [1]

QUESTIONS TO CONSIDER:

○ WHAT CONCERNS AM I DEALING WITH RIGHT NOW?

○ WHAT ELSE IS ADDING TO THE OVERWHELM IN THIS SEASON (SCHEDULES, CHANGES, RELATIONSHIPS, RESPONSIBILITIES, ETC)?

○ ARE ANY OF MY HABITS CONTRIBUTING TO THIS NEGATIVE STRESS?

○ WHAT AM I ALREADY DOING TO ALLEVIATE PRESSURE AND STRESS?

___
___
___
___
___
___
___
___
___
___
___

Instead of grasping at all these issues out of my reach, He's teaching me to bring them down to earth where I can put them under authority and see them for what they are.

I'm learning to nail them down. I just use my old journal, but I don't think you don't have to be a writer to do this.

The stress, sickness, chaos, and deadlines get filtered onto the paper, one thing at a time. As I write each thing down, big and small, they're caught and pinned. They might squirm a little but they're not going anywhere, and I can look them in the eye and rest again. And when I read it later (in admittedly awful handwriting) they're all brought down, down, down to the right size. [2]

It's completely honest, nothing fancy. Pure, rough, unrefined, like the tree that He nailed everything to 2000 years ago. It is us, hushed, listening for Him. It is praying on paper. He speaks when we listen, and for me, the clutter is quieter and He is louder when I write it out. The Spirit falls and the Son is magnified. All those issues come down a peg, brought down to size before the One who really knows what to do about all of it.

It's significant that paper is made from the same material He was nailed to. He still uses it to heal us, show us more of Him, and conquer what's harassing us. [3]

He is not afraid of bad news; his heart is firm, trusting in the Lord. His heart is steady; he will not be afraid, until he looks in triumph on his adversaries.

- Psalm 112:7-8

Our usual response when we come under attack is to pray directly for the situation. If we get sick, we pray to get better. If we're struggling with finances, we pray for provision. If we're in a hard relationship, we pray for wisdom and healing. It makes sense. Of course we want to strike back at the same place the enemy is attacking.

But when we deal with spiritual attack from spiritual enemies (whether they are working through humans or something else entirely) sometimes the obvious answer doesn't always work; it seems to persist no matter how much or often we strike it with prayer.

A while ago a friend shared a strategy I'd never heard of, called "prayer trigger, prayer target." It made no sense at all to me at first: You experience attack in one area, and you respond not by praying for that, but by choosing something completely unrelated to intercede for every time it happens. Something big. Just a quick prayer, steadily fired, each time you deal with that attack.

Weird, hmm? Sort of a different tack on "resist the enemy and he will flee from you" – play it cool and use it as a reminder to intercede in a big way. So I tried it. And as weeks went by, I saw huge moves in both the area I was praying for and in the area I was attacked in. [4]

QUESTIONS TO CONSIDER:

◯ WHAT PERSISTENT ATTACK HAVE I BEEN DEALING WITH IN SPITE OF MY PRAYERS AGAINST IT?

◯ WHAT UNRELATED, BIG THING CAN I TRY PRAYING FOR INSTEAD?

_____
_____
_____
_____
_____
_____
_____
_____

It could be that we're continuing to pray for our circumstances not out of belief, but out of unbelief. Do we really believe God heard us? It still hurts, it's still broken, so do we really trust that He is already taking care of it? Or are we the child who was already given a favorable answer but keeps coming back to ask the same question over and over anyway, not believing their parent is really going to follow through? 5

QUESTIONS TO CONSIDER:

○ DO I REALLY BELIEVE GOD HAS HEARD ME, OR THAT HE CARES?

○ HAS HE ALREADY ANSWERED ME? OR, DO I BELIEVE THAT HE WILL?

○ HOW CAN I SHIFT MY THINKING AND PRAYING FROM ASKING FROM A PLACE OF DOUBT TO ASKING FROM A PLACE OF FAITH?

It's true that sometimes we need to continue to pray for a particular situation; Jesus prayed twice for a man to receive his sight. You might also remember that He told the parable of a persistent widow knocking repeatedly at a judge's door for justice – which many apply as reason to continue in prayer, though it's actually a contrast between an unrighteous judge who eventually listens to the woman out of frustration, versus God our Father speedily giving "justice to His elect who cry out to Him day and night."

> *I tell you, he will give justice to them speedily. Nevertheless, when the Son of Man comes, will he find faith on earth?*
>
> *- Luke 18:8*

We might need to keep praying. But we also need to examine our hearts to see if we're continuing to pray the same thing because we need to, or if it's because we don't trust Him to answer us in the first place. [5]

It might be that we need to just thank Him for hearing and answering us, because He repeatedly tells us He will. [6]

> *Again I say to you, if two of you agree on earth about anything they ask, it will be done for them by my Father in heaven.*
>
> *- Matthew 18:19*
>
> *When the disciples saw it, they marveled, saying, "How did the fig tree wither at once?" And Jesus answered them, "Truly, I say to you, if you have faith and do not doubt, you will not only do what has been done to the fig tree, but even if you say to this mountain, 'Be taken up and thrown into the sea,' it will happen. And whatever you ask in prayer, you will receive, if you have faith."*
>
> *- Matthew 21:20-22*

SUGGESTED SCRIPTURE TO LOOK UP AND COPY: MARK 11:24, JOHN 14:13, JOHN 15:7, JOHN 15:16, JOHN 16:23-24, JAMES 1:5-6, JAMES 1:17, 1 JOHN 3:22, AND 1 JOHN 5:14-15.

_____
_____
_____
_____
_____
_____
_____
_____
_____
_____
_____
_____
_____
_____
_____
_____
_____

It might be that once we've prayed about it, we need to trust Him to move beyond what we can see and then go on to pray for other things.

> *Search me, O God, and know my heart! Try me and know my thoughts!*
>
> *- Psalm 139:23*

What we think we know can get in the way of what we need to know – and what we need to know is that God is big enough to take care of this situation and bring total redemption to it.

In the meantime, we can believe for wild healing and restoration for someone else, and watch Him move on behalf of both of us. Our victory is here. [7]

What would happen if those darkest, most hopeless places, institutions, and people were tackled in prayer on a level that no one has had the grit and persistence to take on before?

What if we prayed – *really* prayed, with bright, life-giving detail – over those who've grown wild, refusing to admit fault, admit reality, admit their own weakness? What if we were brave enough to picture what it would look like if the darkest businesses were replaced with those that breathed life in a community – and then we prayed it into existence? [8]

The light yoke of responsibility, maturity, and surrender are only a breath away. The heavy yoke of filth and blackness costs so much, and lies to those who are in it that the effort to take the deep breath of surrender isn't worth it. What if we made the road smoother through prayer that refuses to give up on them?

I've also been the one who was lost, and losing, and needed someone to fight in prayer for me. Many of us would not be who we are today without those who fought the darkness for us. [9]

QUESTIONS TO CONSIDER:

○ WHO HAS HELPED PRAY ME INTO MATURITY?

○ HOW HAVE I NEEDED PEOPLE TO PRAY FOR ME?

○ WHO NEEDS ME TO PRAY FOR THEM, AND HOW CAN I PICTURE THE VICTORY FOR THEM IN PRAYER?

○ WHAT AREA IN THE NEIGHBORHOOD, COMMUNITY, COUNTRY, GOVERNMENT, OR WORLD CAN I PRAY LIFE AND HEALTH INTO?

_____
_____
_____
_____
_____
_____
_____
_____
_____
_____
_____
_____
_____
_____
_____

We have loved ones stuck in this kind of mire, and this is where the fight comes in for those of us who love them and are tempted to just wash our hands and give up on them. Giving up seems easier to us, just as it seems to them, because the pain of disappointment after raised hopes is so hard to bear.

But this stubborn, unyielding prayer is where we fight, because the decision between hope and despair is where the battle rages. This is where the outcome of victory or defeat is decided. And we should take someone with us, because even spiritual proximity to the morass can threaten to suck us under, too. We can be the powerful loving ones, clinging to a healthy vision of the one who is lost in darkness, refusing to let it go. [10]

Be sober-minded; be watchful. Your adversary the devil prowls around like a roaring lion, seeking someone to devour. Resist him, firm in your faith, knowing that the same kinds of suffering are being experienced by your brotherhood throughout the world.

- 1 Peter 5:8-9

We cling to this hope and pray it into existence regardless of the blackness that pulses and threatens. We could fade away and give up, but heroes run into the battle and not away from it. Our loved ones need us to be those heroes – because they too are meant to be heroes, and that's why the enemy fights so desperately for them.

That enemy whispers, "Give up. Lower your weapons."

And we respond, "Fire." [11]

Sometimes it's all I can do just to keep our kids from throwing toys at each other or sabotaging each other's toothbrushes; I struggle to wrap my mind around the bigger, broader issues outside our door. And I even feel guilty for praying for comparatively small needs in our home when there are immensely huge events happening out there.

It feels urgent, like we have to choose – and what if something tragic is happening to issue B while I'm still praying over issue A?

That's just me. You are probably far more calm and level-headed about all this.

I catch myself slipping into this different kind of fear, an anxiety over prayer – which is ridiculous, since that's the opposite of what prayer should accomplish – and it takes me a while to realize that it's just another ploy of the enemy to make something productive and powerful seem burdensome and impotent.

And that's a lie. The enemy is a liar who is afraid of God's people praying. He will do whatever he can to convince us not to do it, which is a very good reason to do it without ceasing. [12]

QUESTIONS TO CONSIDER:

◯ WHAT LIES HAVE I BELIEVED THAT HAVE HINDERED ME FROM PRAYING WITHOUT CEASING?

◯ WHAT IS THE ACTUAL TRUTH?

_____
_____
_____
_____
_____
_____
_____
_____
_____
_____
_____
_____
_____
_____

Like most lies and doubts, the lie that states our prayer isn't powerful enough, or fast enough, or covering enough is a half-truth. It's true that terrible things happen all over the world and we can't possibly pray over everything at once with the proper urgency to pick them all off one at a time, as though we were playing some sort of spiritual Galaga.

But it is also true that you and I don't have to think of everything or be in control of everything. This fear and anxiety is not all that different from what causes my son to sabotage and give up on his relationships with his family – both stem from an unhealthy need for control and a distrust in the One in authority to be able to handle the hard things within and around us. Like a good parent, we can trust God to teach us to listen for and obey His promptings, and we can trust Him to deal with everything we can't take care of at any given moment.

Because it is also true that God is not limited to our time frame. [13]

> *If you picture Time as a straight line along which we have to travel, then you must picture God as the whole page on which the line is drawn. We come to the parts of the line one by one: we have to leave A behind before we get to B, and cannot reach C until we leave B behind. God, from above or outside or all round, contains the whole line, and sees it all.*
>
> *– C.S. Lewis* [14]

Being filled with truth, knowing we are covered by Jesus' righteousness, protects us from fear and anxiety. Once we disarm fear with faith, we can go anywhere in prayer He calls us. We move from defense to offense and follow the promptings He gives us. [15]

> *In all circumstances take up the shield of faith, with which you can extinguish all the flaming darts of the evil one; and take the helmet of salvation, and the sword of the Spirit, which is the word of God, praying at all times in the Spirit, with all prayer and supplication.*
>
> *– Ephesians 6:16-18a*

QUESTIONS TO CONSIDER:

◯ HOW DOES MY PERSPECTIVE SHIFT WHEN I PRAY FROM FAITH INSTEAD OF FROM FEAR?

◯ WHAT PROMPTINGS HAS GOD BEEN GIVING ME IN PRAYER?

◯ WHAT HAVE I NOTICED LATELY THAT I NORMALLY WOULD NOT PAY ATTENTION TO?

_____
_____
_____
_____
_____
_____
_____
_____
_____
_____
_____
_____
_____
_____
_____
_____

As we pursue prayer in the offhand moments, He teaches us to notice things we never would have on our own. We look out the window and instead of just staring at the leaves whipping across the street, we intercede for the neighbor who lives there. We watch the leaves shoot upward and we pray for her house, her safety, her warmth through the winter. We pray for the neighbors to be kind, patient, and gracious to each other. We pray for a sense of community, respect, and camaraderie. And there goes the neighborhood. [16]

Our countries are in dire need of Jesus. Our leaders need wisdom and repentance just like we do, our towns and cities need protection just like our homes, businesses, churches, and schools do – and we can pray for any of them without fearing that we're missing something urgent to avoid tragedy.

Our nations are at a pivotal moment, and our prayers for small things and big things make a difference. He hears and moves because prayer is powerful and productive. Years from now, we will look back on these days and know that we saved lives and slew monsters through relentless intercession. [16]

To that end keep alert with all perseverance, making supplication for all the saints, and also for me, that words may be given to me in opening my mouth boldly to proclaim the mystery of the gospel, for which I am an ambassador in chains, that I may declare it boldly, as I ought to speak.

– Ephesians 6:18b-20

In the beginning was the Word, and the Word was with God, and the Word was God. He was in the beginning with God. All things were made through him, and without him was not any thing made that was made. In him was life, and the life was the light of men.

– John 1:1-4

He tells us to pray in ways that simultaneously prevent events from happening and create things into being.

We are learning the relentless, without-ceasing part: During a sermon, interceding for the pastor and our hearts as we listen; during conversation, changing a one-on-one discussion into a conference call with God, whether the other person knows it or not; during our reading and study as we talk to God about the words on the page and discern whether or not they align with truth. [17]

QUESTIONS TO CONSIDER:

◯ WHAT IS GOD ASKING ME TO HELP BRING TO LIFE IN THIS SEASON?

◯ WHAT DOES RELENTLESS PRAYER LOOK LIKE IN THE DIFFERENT MOMENTS OF MY DAY?

_____
_____
_____
_____
_____
_____
_____
_____
_____
_____
_____
_____
_____
_____

The light shines in the darkness, and the darkness has not overcome it.

– John 1:5

Throughout the day we're praying, and not just in the quiet available moments. During laundry, during the commute, during the phone call with the specialist – we're asking, *Lord, what are Your words here?* And He's right there, waking us up to bring light into dark places. We get to help make the headlines, and lights are turning on everywhere. [18]

7: light

But God does not call his people simply to run around putting out fires after the secular world has lighted them. He calls us to light our own fires, to renew culture.

Charles Colson [1]

I'm learning to pray that God would be cleaning us as I clean the house. As I'm scrubbing grime around the sink faucets, I'm asking Him to remove calcified areas and hardening stubbornness. Dusting neglected areas, I'm asking Him to reveal what needs attention and care. Folding towels, I'm thanking Him for clean water and healthy bodies, and praying for those who have neither. While sorting boys clothes on one side of the couch and girls clothes on the other, I'm praying that these kids would be grateful for what they have, steward their things well, and not be immature whiners. And I'm praying that for me, too.

Our relentless prayer is behind the scenes, life-transforming, future-changing, people-saving work, but it's not glittering and sophisticated. It's rugged, rustic, primitive – beautiful in humility, sincerity, and imperfection. It is the movement underground that builds until the earth shakes.

It's not just requests and intercession. It's not just praise and thankfulness. Mostly, it's His presence encompassing every type of prayer, like music that permeates every room of a house. [2]

QUESTIONS TO CONSIDER:

○ HOW CAN I PRAY THROUGH THE DETAILS OF A TYPICAL DAY?

○ HOW ARE MY REQUESTS, INTERCESSION, PRAISE, AND THANKFULNESS CHANGING THE WORLD AROUND ME?

○ HOW AM I RECOGNIZING HIS PRESENCE WITH ME IN EVERY MOMENT?

○ IF I'M NOT RECOGNIZING HIS PRESENCE EVERY DAY, WHERE CAN I BEGIN? WHAT ARE SOME BABY STEPS I CAN TAKE IN THAT DIRECTION?

_____

_____

_____

Whatever you do, work heartily, as for the Lord and not for men, knowing that from the Lord you will receive the inheritance as your reward. You are serving the Lord Christ.

– Colossians 3:23-24

Let your speech always be gracious, seasoned with salt, so that you may know how you ought to answer each person.

- Colossians 4:6

Every conversation we engage in changes or maintains the atmosphere of our home, office, ministry, and community, for better or worse. Whatever the season or temperature outside, the way we speak determines if it's warm or cool inside. Our words and tone keep us close to each other or push us apart.

Our conversations can leave others full or empty, in rain or shine.

It's not always easy. Life is messy, full of tough situations and emotional topics that require heaps of wisdom and self-control in order to keep our conversations filled with grace. [3]

QUESTIONS TO CONSIDER:

○ WHAT HAS THE ATMOSPHERE BEEN LIKE AROUND ME LATELY? HOW ARE MY WORDS AND TONE CONTRIBUTING TO IT?

○ WHAT SITUATIONS AM I DEALING WITH THAT ARE CHALLENGING ME THE MOST IN THIS? HOW DO I SEE GOD MOVING IN THESE SAME SITUATIONS?

○ WHAT IS GOD TELLING ME ABOUT MY OWN NEED FOR GRACE, WISDOM, SELF-CONTROL, GENTLENESS, AND PATIENCE?

○ WHERE IS GOD TELLING ME TO EXTEND GRACE, WISDOM, SELF-CONTROL, GENTLENESS, AND PATIENCE?

_____
_____
_____
_____
_____
_____
_____
_____
_____

Preach the word; be ready in season and out of season; reprove, rebuke, and exhort, with complete patience and teaching.

- 2 Timothy 4:2

Questions to consider:

- What are the definitions of reprove, rebuke, and exhort?
- Why are these three words used together?
- What is God saying to me through this verse?

Put on then, as God's chosen ones, holy and beloved, compassionate hearts, kindness, humility, meekness, and patience.

- Colossians 3:12

Sometimes I'm the one who requires endless amounts of correction and teaching. He speaks, and the air around me starts to thaw.

Talk to Me, Love, He says. *Just like a little kid who talks to her parents incessantly, you need to talk to Me. I'm here to fill you all day long, because when you're hydrated with the Living Water, I can speak through you. You won't dry up, you won't get cold, and you'll never run on empty.*

He only calls us to speak to others the same way He speaks to us. [4]

QUESTIONS TO CONSIDER:

○ WHAT DOES IT LOOK LIKE FOR ME TO PUT ON A COMPASSIONATE HEART, KINDNESS, HUMILITY, MEEKNESS, AND PATIENCE?

○ WHAT CURRENT SITUATION(S) DO I MOST NEED TO DO THAT WITH?

○ HOW MIGHT DOING SO CHANGE THE DETAILS AND OUTCOME OF THAT SITUATION?

    Our home, like yours maybe, has several work stations. The dining table doubles as a school desk, an ancient sideboard holds our computer, and the kitchen is often on duty from nine in the morning to well past midnight. But there's one particular area that holds most of my affection – my family generously calls it "Mom's work table" although to be honest, there's almost no table to be seen underneath the mess of yarn and papers on top of it. Projects, craft stuff, books, a bazillion works in progress. Sometimes they even get finished.

    But some days it all seems so trivial.

    I get tired of the headlines. They are so big, and we are so small. We grieve and rage and share and pray and give money and still, the headlines keep coming, relentless.

    What do we do in the face of such events? Disasters, persecution, and cruelty of epic proportions occurred throughout the centuries, but what makes our time period unique is that earlier generations never dealt with the onslaught of information overload of multiple tragedies occurring simultaneously all over the world. [5]

QUESTIONS TO CONSIDER:

◯ WHAT GIFTINGS AND INTERESTS HAS GOD GIVEN ME THAT I SOMETIMES FEEL GUILTY FOR INDULGING IN?

◯ WHAT CAUSES, NEEDS, AND CURRENT EVENTS AM I PASSIONATE ABOUT?

◯ HOW DO MY GIFTINGS, INTERESTS, AND PASSIONS REFLECT THE HEART OF GOD AND HIS DESIGN FOR ME?

_____

_____

_____

_____

_____

_____

_____

When there are orphans needing families, people grieving, bodies hurting, and communities desperate for truth, why do I put so much time into the projects on my table? What good is reading, writing, rearranging bookshelves, or crocheting an afghan? Why should we spend time painting, or playing music, or, well, *steam cleaning the carpet* (if we're going to be really honest) when there is a culture to transform?

He answers, *Because there **is** a culture to transform, Love. That's exactly why. Your life and the details in it are a witness to others about My Kingdom. It's all ministry.*

He knows the joy in creating intricate detail, constructing beauty where before there was only ugliness and disorder. [6]

Christianity alone has the resources to restore the arts to their proper place, for Christianity is a worldview that supports human creativity yet does so with appropriate humility. Made in the image of the Creator, humans find fulfillment in being creative in their own sphere. Yet unlike God, the human artist does not create out of nothing.

- Charles Colson [7]

The same God who loves the orphan and heals the dying is also the Designer concerned with the finest veins on a leaf, the stripes on a housecat, and the changes wrought in every season. He knows why we enjoy sewing stitches, composing music, and making paint strokes and key strokes.

We imitate our Father in the creator/designer aspect that is innovative and beautiful. We also reflect Him in the healer/redeemer role that is passionate, nurturing, world changing, and in the trenches.

And both sides are necessary. Too much time focused on aesthetics leaves us aloof and ignorant, and too much time entrenched in warfare leaves us burned out and bitter. [8]

QUESTIONS TO CONSIDER:

- HOW DO I REFLECT GOD IN HIS CREATOR/DESIGNER ASPECT?
- HOW DO I REFLECT HIM IN HIS HEALER/REDEEMER ROLE?
- DO I TEND MORE TOWARD ONE CHARACTERISTIC THAN THE OTHER?

But one more thing is needed to keep us in healthy equilibrium between the two, without which any light we attempt to create is blown out.

His presence is fire. Without it, no light. Our imitation of Him is only a puff of hot air if we aren't actually spending time with Him.

Hunkered down in His presence, our gifts press out and expand the Kingdom. We influence the culture through high quality works of excellence that command and deserve attention, *Soli Deo Gloria* style. [9]

> *To work from large interests and a desire for great activity and world movements, to the inner circle life with Me, is really the wrong way. That is why so often, when...a soul finds Me, I have to begin our Friendship by cutting away the ties that bind it to the outer and wider circle. When it has gained strength and learned its lesson in the inner circle, it can then widen its life, working this time from within out, taking then to each contact, each friendship, the inner circle influence.*
>
> *And this is to be your way of life.*
>
> *This is the way of the Spirit.* [10]

Love one another with brotherly affection.

Outdo one another in showing honor.

Do not be slothful in zeal, be fervent in the Spirit, serve the Lord.

Rejoice in hope, be patient in tribulation, be constant in prayer.

Contribute to the needs of the saints and seek to show hospitality.

- Romans 12:10-13

QUESTIONS TO CONSIDER:

○ HOW AM I CURRENTLY LIVING THIS OUT?

○ ARE THERE ANY WAYS I WANT TO LIVE THIS OUT DIFFERENTLY?

ARE THERE HABITS, ROUTINES, OR OTHER THINGS I NEED TO CHANGE IN ORDER TO DO SO?

_____
_____
_____
_____
_____
_____
_____
_____
_____
_____
_____
_____
_____
_____
_____
_____
_____

Love, in kindness – it can change someone's day, which then changes their future.

Love, in righteous anger – self-controlled, quiet, and motivating.

Love, in education – refusing to give in to apathy, ignorance, or laziness. We are not those who shrink back.

Love, in generosity – because He has modeled extravagance to us.

Love, in hope – not wishful thinking, but confident knowing and patient creativity.

Love, in prayer – above all else, unceasing, relentless, and effective.

Love, in worship – because we know Who we are dealing with. [11]

The distractions buzz around a wind-smeared August sky, creating more noise. In the rapidly waning summer, I removed commitments my heart was no longer fully behind, because those endeavors were a burden no longer authorized by the Spirit and I let go of them in order to walk through the threshold. *All things are lawful, but not all things build up* – and this is a time that requires building.

Each gift used from His presence is a fire, full of grace and beauty, yet uncompromising in truth. Our culture sees Him by the light of it and is transformed. [11]

QUESTIONS TO CONSIDER:

○ ARE THERE ANY COMMITMENTS OR DISTRACTIONS GOD HAS BEEN TELLING ME TO RELEASE IN ORDER TO BUILD IN THIS NEW SEASON? HOW AM I GOING TO DO THAT?

○ HOW DO I SEE THE CULTURE AND COMMUNITY AROUND ME TRANSFORMED BY THE GIFTS GOD GIVES HIS PEOPLE? HOW DO I WANT TO LEAN INTO THAT?

○ WHAT IDEAS, INNOVATIONS, OR DREAMS HAS GOD GIVEN ME THAT NO ONE ELSE HAS STEPPED INTO YET? IS GOD ASKING ME TO BREAK GROUND IN A COMPLETELY NEW AREA? HOW CAN I START PURSUING THAT?

_____
_____
_____
_____
_____
_____
_____
_____
_____

As for what was sown on good soil, this is the one who hears the word and understands it. He indeed bears fruit and yields, in one case a hundredfold, in another sixty, and in another thirty.

– Matthew 13:23

And we are His dust, partnered with Daylight. The harvest comes from His presence in us, never sleeping.

There's a time and a place for loud declarations, but most of our influence – the fruit we bear – comes from the quiet, persistent attendance of Jesus in every area of our lives. Not by painting crosses on everything we make, but by pursuing the giftings and talents He created us with and then using them boldly, wisely, and well in every sphere He puts us. [12]

What we want is not more little books about Christianity, but more little books by Christians on other subjects – with their Christianity latent.

– C.S. Lewis [13]

It's Christianity that is not shushed or hidden, but inherent. It's Jesus permeating everything through His people, even on a cloudy day when sin and mosquitoes are everywhere discouraging us.

He's leaving no stone unturned in the tilling as we partner with Him in the harvest. And we bear healthier fruit when we enrich our soil – filling ourselves with His words and educating ourselves with great works of His people. We're not looking for just anything we can get our hands on; we're using our time and resources strategically to guard and prepare our hearts. We want a vast array of nourishing, challenging, truth-filled content that grows and inspires us. [14]

QUESTIONS TO CONSIDER:

○ HOW AM I ENRICHING MY SOIL? HOW AM I INVESTING IN MY OWN EDUCATION?

○ HOW CAN I USE MY TIME AND RESOURCES MORE STRATEGICALLY?

○ WHAT BOOKS, AUTHORS, OR OTHER RESOURCES DO I WANT TO DELVE FURTHER INTO?

_____

_____

_____

_____

_____

_____

_____

_____

_____

_____

Keep your heart with all vigilance, for from it flow the springs of life.

– *Proverbs 4:23*

But we also need rest. Like soil, we need downtime or we get depleted and nothing can grow from us. We need firm boundaries from buzzing negativity that harasses and discourages us. We need dates with our spouse, Sabbaths, and occasional afternoon breaks behind a locked door with a clandestine bar of chocolate that isn't shared with the kids. At least, I do. [14]

> *And He said to them, "Come away by yourselves to a desolate place and rest a while." For many were coming and going, and they had no leisure even to eat.*
>
> *– Mark 6:31*

QUESTIONS TO CONSIDER:

○ AM I RESTING ENOUGH? ARE THERE BOUNDARIES I NEED TO PUT IN PLACE TO CREATE MORE MARGIN?

○ HOW CAN I TELL WHEN I'M STARTING TO GET DEPLETED?

○ WHAT BIG OR SMALL THINGS DO I NEED TO PRIORITIZE TO KEEP ME FROM RUNNING ON EMPTY? HOW CAN I DO THAT IN THIS SEASON?

___
___
___
___
___
___
___
___
___
___
___
___

We're meant to bear exceptional fruit, not just low-quality filler taking up space and adding to the noise. We're made to pour out our gifts in a way that reflects the excellent nature of the original Creator – generously, without fear, and trusting Him with the results. When we do, it creates a culture that can't ignore the Light permeating it. [15]

> *The good person out of the good treasure of his heart produces good, and the evil person out of his evil treasure produces evil, for out of the abundance of the heart his mouth speaks.*
>
> *– Luke 6:45*

But I tend to second-guess a lot of things. The mission is hard. Some stuff looks like it's not working out, and other situations look like they're falling apart entirely. Do you feel this, friends?

We chant this refrain of, *God, what have we done? If we were doing it right, surely it would be working...we must be doing something wrong...should I hit the undo button? Or should I just highlight the whole shebang and hit delete?*

I check, and look, and doubt progress, forgetting that completing the work takes a million keystrokes. Much is happening under the surface. [16]

> *Likewise the Spirit helps us in our weakness. For we do not know what to pray for as we ought, but the Spirit himself intercedes for us with groanings too deep for words. And he who searches hearts knows what is the mind of the Spirit, because the Spirit intercedes for the saints according to the will of God.*
>
> *– Romans 8:26-27*

QUESTIONS TO CONSIDER:

○ WHAT SITUATIONS AM I DEALING WITH THAT LOOK LIKE THEY'RE FALTERING OR FEEL LIKE FAILURE?

○ HAVE I OBEYED FULLY IN THEM?

○ WHAT MIGHT BE HAPPENING UNDER THE SURFACE?

*And the Lord said to Joshua, "See, **I have given Jericho into your hand**, with its king and mighty men of valor. **You shall march around the city**, all the men of war going around the city once. **Thus shall you do for six days.** Seven priests shall bear seven trumpets of rams' horns before the ark. **On the seventh day you shall march around the city seven times**, and the priests shall blow the trumpets.*

– Joshua 6:2-4

The instructions are specific. We know which direction we're going and what we're supposed to do once we get there. So why isn't it working?

Stop counting steps, He tells me. *Just count the laps and don't overthink it. The truth is, Love, that wall is coming down – it's just that you've only walked around it three or four times.* [17]

> *Enemy-occupied territory – that is what this world is. Christianity is the story of how the rightful king has landed, you might say landed in disguise, and is calling us all to take part in a great campaign of sabotage.*
>
> *– C.S. Lewis* [18]

If we are in obedience and things still seem to be falling apart, we might be right where He wants us: heavily engaged, typing away, focused on the mission at hand, not missing the forest for the trees. Those on the front lines come under the heaviest fire, and each of our positions is a strategic assignment.

> *And at the seventh time, when the priests had blown the trumpets, Joshua said to the people, "Shout, for the Lord has given you the city."*
>
> *– Joshua 6:16*

Our obedience – steadfast, unwavering, swerving neither to the right nor left – is one of the greatest threats to the enemy. Combined with worship, it liberates captives and takes the city. [19]

_____

_____

_____

_____

_____

_____

_____

_____

_____

_____

_____

_____

_____

This day does not define you. The questions, assumptions, and judgments of others do not define you. Your children's behavior does not define you.

What about...?

Nope. Not your biological kids, either.

Even when their behavior is a reflection of yours – whether good or bad – it doesn't define who you are. I'm moving in every part of this. Not a moment, not a situation is wasted. [20]

QUESTIONS TO CONSIDER:

○ WHAT HAVE I ALLOWED TO DEFINE ME? WHAT TRULY DEFINES ME?

○ WHAT IS GOD ACCOMPLISHING IN MY HARD DAYS?

Do you remember a year ago?
And I answer, Must I? Do I really have to?
I know. Some things were better. Most were much more difficult.

Those things that you are discouraged by, those things that seem to be in limbo with no progress, only seem the same on the surface. They are about to transform like a rapidly blooming desert flower that will remain unfading because My work is everlasting in you and in those you love.

You need to do more than picture the victory now, Love. You need to expect it.

QUESTIONS TO CONSIDER:

○ HOW HAVE I SEEN GOD MOVE IN MY LIFE OVER THE LAST YEAR?

○ HOW HAS GOD USED ME IN THE LIVES OF OTHERS OVER THE LAST YEAR?

○ WHAT DOES IT LOOK LIKE FOR ME TO EXPECT THE VICTORY OVER THE COMING YEAR?

These days of listening for Him are like gathering manna – knowing that I have no words without His provision, but trusting Him to lay the pieces out for me every day to find and pick up. And He always does. They're not always where I think they are; sometimes they take longer to put together than I'd like. We all want answers for our questions...but we also want to have a say in the answers we get.

Sometimes He's the one gathering up the pieces for us. Sometimes we fall into pieces from the happenings of the day, the test results, the phone call, and He pulls us together again, taking every scheme of the enemy and turning it on its head for our good, and His goodness. [21]

> *And we know that for those who love God all things work together for good, for those who are called according to his purpose.*
>
> *– Romans 8:28*

He picks up our pieces and gives them back to us, but they will be transformed, and so will we. He'll say, *This peace is for you. And in this hurtful situation, this peace is for you. And this act of forgiveness, and this gesture of kindness, and all of these moves in obedience...they are for you, too.* **This peace is for you.**

The real masterpiece is His child, refined though maturity and surrender. His people, trained for battle and victory. [22]

Notes

Introduction

1. Kenneth Grahame, *The Wind in the Willows* (New York: Sterling Publishing Co., 2005), 134.

Chapter 1: Abiding

1. Brother Lawrence, *The Practice of the Presence of God* (Peabody, Mass: Hendrickson Publishers, 2004), 22.
2. Shannon Guerra, *Oh My Soul* (Wasilla, Alaska: Copperlight Wood, 2018), 13-14.
3. Ibid, 15.
4. Ibid, 20.
5. Ibid, 21.

Chapter 2: Identity

1. Madeleine L'Engle, *A Circle of Quiet* (San Francisco: HarperCollins, 1972), 233.
2. Shannon Guerra, *Oh My Soul* (Wasilla, Alaska: Copperlight Wood, 2018), 29.
3. Ibid, 32.
4. Ibid, 33-34.
5. Ibid, 35.
6. Ibid, 38.
7. Jerry Bridges, *The Pursuit of Holiness* (Colorado Springs: NavPress, 2006), 80.
8. *Oh My Soul*, 38-39.
9. Ibid, 42.
10. Ibid, 42-43.
11. Ibid, 45.
12. Ibid, 47.

Chapter 3: Threshold

1. Shannon Guerra, *Oh My Soul* (Wasilla, Alaska: Copperlight Wood, 2018), 51.
2. Ibid, 53.
3. Ibid, 54.
4. Ibid, 56.
5. Ibid, 58.
6. Ibid, 58-59.
7. Ibid, 60.
8. Ibid, 61.
9. Ibid, 62.
10. Ibid, 63.
11. Ibid, 68.

Chapter 4: Forward

1. Shannon Guerra, *Oh My Soul* (Wasilla, Alaska: Copperlight Wood, 2018), 78-79.
2. Ibid, 81.
3. Ibid, 83-84.
4. Ibid, 87.
5. Ibid, 89.
6. Ibid, 90.
7. Ibid, 93.
8. Ibid, 94.
9. Ibid, 96.
10. Ibid, 96-97.

Chapter 5: Friendship

1. Shannon Guerra, *Oh My Soul* (Wasilla, Alaska: Copperlight Wood, 2018), 101.
2. Ibid, 102.
3. Ibid, 105.
4. Ibid, 105-106.
5. Ibid, 106.
6. Ibid, 108.
7. Ibid, 113.
8. Ibid, 113-114.
9. Ibid, 116.
10. Kenneth Grahame, *The Wind in the Willows* (New York: Sterling Publishing Co., 2005), 48.

Chapter 6: Fire

1. Shannon Guerra, *Oh My Soul* (Wasilla, Alaska: Copperlight Wood, 2018), 121-122.
2. Ibid, 122.
3. Ibid, 122-123.
4. Ibid, 123-124.
5. Ibid, 127.
6. Ibid, 127-128.
7. Ibid, 128.
8. Ibid, 129-130.
9. Ibid, 130.
10. Ibid, 130-131.
11. Ibid, 131.
12. Ibid, 133.
13. Ibid, 133-134.
14. C.S. Lewis, *Mere Christianity* (New York: MacMillan Publishing Company, 1952), 147.
15. Shannon Guerra, *Oh My Soul* (Wasilla, Alaska: Copperlight Wood, 2018), 134.
16. Ibid, 135.
17. Ibid, 137.
18. Ibid, 137-138.

Chapter 7: Light

1. Charles Colson, *How Now Shall We Live?* (Wheaton, Ill: Tyndale Publishers, 1999), 450.
2. Shannon Guerra, *Oh My Soul* (Wasilla, Alaska: Copperlight Wood, 2018), 141-142.
3. Ibid, 144.
4. Ibid, 147.
5. Ibid, 149-150.
6. Ibid, 150-151.
7. Charles Colson, *How Now Shall We Live?* (Wheaton, Ill: Tyndale Publishers, 1999), 449.
8. Shannon Guerra, *Oh My Soul* (Wasilla, Alaska: Copperlight Wood, 2018), 151-152.
9. Ibid, 152.
10. *God Calling*, ed. A.J. Russell (Ulrichsville, Ohio: Barbour Publishing, 1998), entry titled "November 28."
11. Shannon Guerra, *Oh My Soul* (Wasilla, Alaska: Copperlight Wood, 2018), 154.
12. Ibid, 156.
13. C.S. Lewis, *The Collected Works of C.S. Lewis*, from the essay "Christian Apologetics" (New York: Inspirational Press, 1996), 362.
14. Shannon Guerra, *Oh My Soul* (Wasilla, Alaska: Copperlight Wood, 2018), 157.
15. Ibid, 158.
16. Ibid, 159-160.
17. Ibid, 160-161.
18. C.S. Lewis, *Mere Christianity* (New York: MacMillan Publishing Company, 1952), 51.
19. Shannon Guerra, *Oh My Soul* (Wasilla, Alaska: Copperlight Wood, 2018), 161.
20. Ibid, 162.
21. Ibid, 162-163.
22. Ibid, 163-164.